Essential Skills in Geography

Rand McNally

Essential Skills in Geography

A Workbook of Basic Geographic Concepts

Rand McNally & Company
Chicago / New York / San Francisco

About the Author

Ann Briscoe Nero, Ed.D., is currently Social Studies Instructional Supervisor for the Memphis City Schools in Memphis, Tennessee. Dr. Nero, a member of the National Council for the Social Studies, and the local Council for the Social Studies, was instrumental in assisting in the development of the K - 12 Social Studies curriculum for the Memphis City schools.

Dr. Nero is a frequent presenter for schools, school districts, and conferences, where she speaks on a variety of topics related to the Social Sciences and the development of critical thinking skills.

About the Editor

Barbara Radner, Ph.D., is an associate professor of education at DePaul University, Chicago. She has developed and edited curriculum materials at the college level, high school level, and for elementary schools in economics, geography, and history and in the physical sciences. As the Director of the Center for Economic Education, Dr. Radner works with educators from Chicago area schools and colleges on the improvement of teaching economics as an integral part of the social sciences.

Fourth Printing 1994
Copyright © 1987 by Rand McNally & Company
All rights reserved
Printed in the United States of America

Contents

Part One /
Developing Skills with Maps

A map is a very special piece of paper. With a map, people have explored faraway places, found their way across thousands of miles of ocean, and even shown where you can see a volcano on a faraway planet. One day, people will use those maps of other planets to find their way traveling on those faraway worlds. Right now you can use maps to explore many places on your own planet. In this part of the workbook, you will practice the skills you need to explore geography with maps.

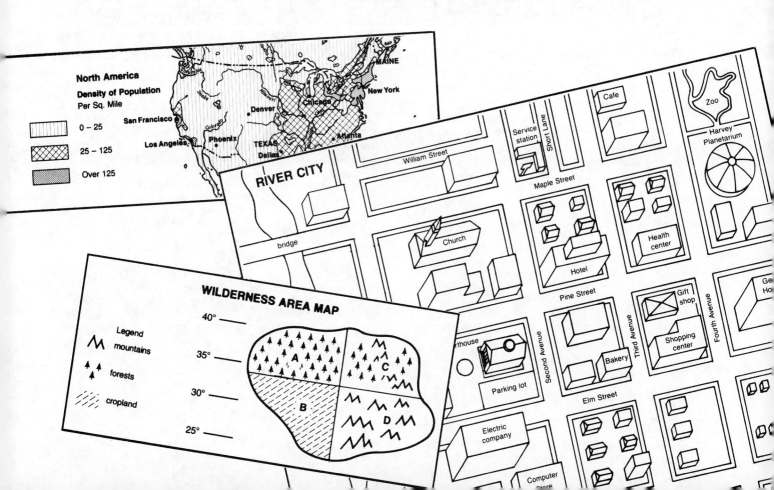

CHAPTER 1: Using Symbols

Every map uses symbols to show the geography of a place. Most maps use lines to show borders and dots to show cities. In these activities, you will learn how to use symbols to explore the geography of cities, states, and countries.

ACTIVITY 1: City Symbols

People use symbols every day. Some symbols show where to find things in a store, other symbols help people drive safely. Before you use symbols to read a map, make your own symbol collection.

Development:

Every city uses signs to show people where places and things are located in the city. They put symbols on those signs and on maps of the city, too. Read these symbols and identify what each one would help people find on a city map.

A.	✈	_____	Railroad
B.	┼┼┼┼┼	_____	Wayside, roadside park
C.	⚑	_____	Airport
D.	⧗	_____	School

Application:

Draw symbols that could stand for each of these places in a city:

_____ Museum   _____ Police station   _____ Hospital

_____ Library   _____ Fire station   _____ Post Office

_____   _____
(add your own)   (add your own)

Keep these symbols; you will use them when you make your own city maps.

ACTIVITY 2: Making a City Map Key

A map key or legend is a kind of chart that shows what the different symbols on a map mean. In this activity you will make up some symbols and put them together in a key for a city map.

Development:

This map shows a part of a small city named River City. There are many different kinds of places in this city, and you will show where they are with symbols.

Draw a symbol for each of the following kinds of stores:

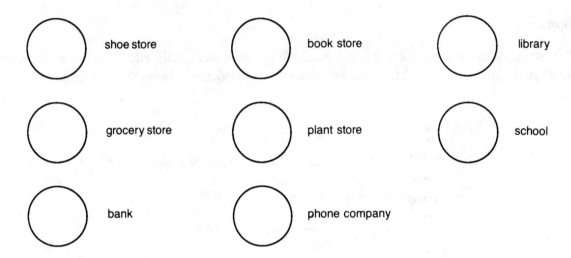

You have made a picture key for the map, and now you should show where each of these places is located. There are circles drawn on the map where your symbols belong. Draw the same symbol you have in your key on the map in the following places. Then insert the letter which identifies each place on the map next to its description below.

_____   The shoe store is at the corner of Maple Street and First Avenue.

_____   The book store is on Pine Street between First and Second Avenues.

_____   The bank is at the corner of Elm Street and Second Avenue.

_____   The phone company is at the northwest corner of Pine Street and Second Avenue.

_____   The library is on Oak Street at Fifth Avenue.

_____   The plant store is on Pine Street across from the hotel.

_____   There are two grocery stores: one at the corner of Maple Street and Second Avenue, the other near the corner of Meadow Lane and Fourth Avenue.

_____   There are two schools: one at the corner of Maple Street and Third Avenue, the other at the corner of Oak Street and First Avenue.

Application:

Make a map that shows several blocks in the neighborhood of your school. Write the names of the streets, and show your school and where other important places in the neighborhood are located. Draw a key that tells what those places are, and use the symbols to show those places on the map.

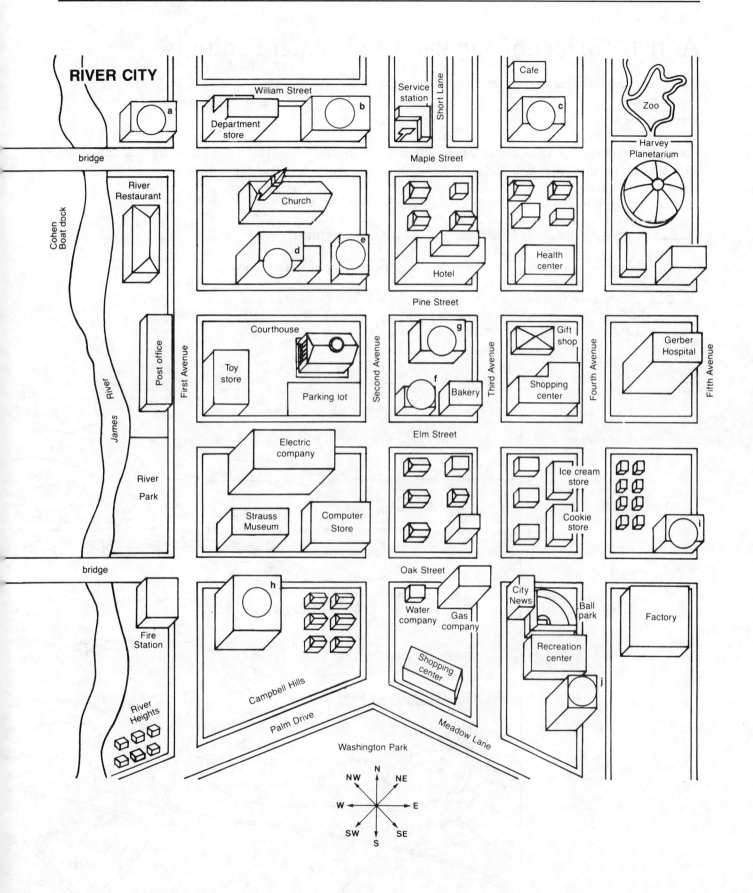

Activity 3: Identifying Land and Water Features

There are many different kinds of land and water features, and this drawing shows some of them.

Development:

For each land or water feature, read the description and then look for the place in the drawing that shows that kind of land or water. When you find that place, write its number next to the description

_____ Bay—Part of a lake or sea that is partly surrounded by land.

_____ Inlet—A small strip of water that reaches from the sea into the shoreland.

_____ Island—Land that is surrounded by water and smaller than a continent.

_____ Isthmus—A narrow piece of land that joins two larger bodies of land.

_____ Lake—A body of water, usually fresh water, that is surrounded by land.

MAP

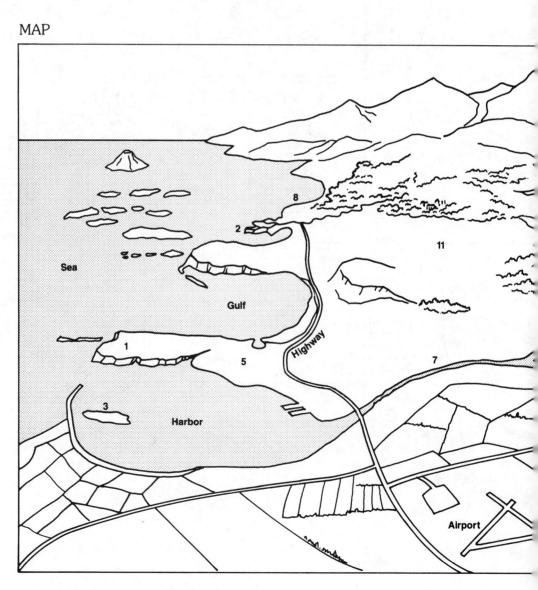

_____ Mountain—Land that rises very high, much higher than the land at its base.

_____ Peninsula—A land area with a narrow link to a larger land area. It is almost surrounded by water.

_____ Plain—A large, flat land area.

_____ River—A large, moving body of fresh water.

_____ Tributary—A stream or small river that flows into a larger river.

_____ Valley—The lower land between hills or mountains.

Application:

Make a picture symbol for each kind of land or water and use your symbols to make a picture symbol key for the map.

Draw your symbol in the space to the left of your numbers.

ACTIVITY 4: Using Highway Symbols on a State Map

When people travel by car, they use maps to choose which roads to use. Symbols on the maps show the different kinds of roads and where they go.

Development:

Use this map of an imaginary state to to figure out what one family saw when they took a trip.

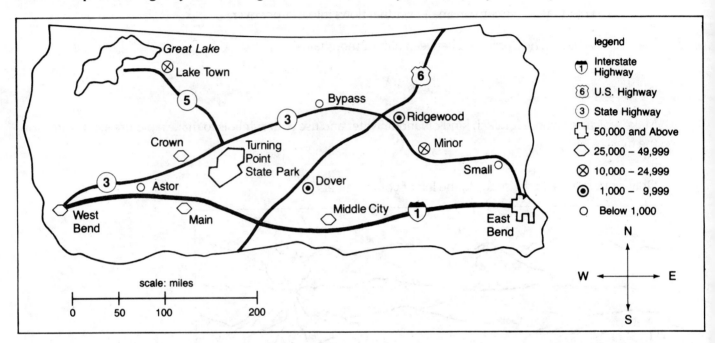

1. The family wanted to go from Crown to West Bend. Which state highway would they drive on to get there?

   _____

2. The family took Interstate Highway 1 from West Bend to East Bend. What two cities did they pass along the way?

   _____   and   _____

3. When the family left East Bend, they went to the town of Small. Just how small is the town of Small? Use the key to find out its population. Look for the symbol used for Small and tell what it means.

   _____

4. When they left Small, they drove to the Great Lake.

   a. What highways did they take?   _____

   b. Name two places they passed along the way.   _____

Application:

Use this map to plan another trip. Then write questions about the trip on a piece of paper and give your questions to another student.

ACTIVITY 5: Using an Elevation Map

Elevation means the height of land above sea level. In this activity you will learn how to use an elevation key so that you can tell just how high or low land is anywhere on the earth.

Development:

Elevation keys use color or lines to show different heights. Use the key to find the heights of different places on this map of the United States.

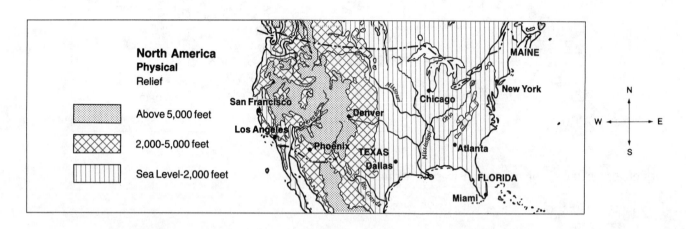

1. How high is the land at Phoenix? _____

2. How high is the land at New York? _____

3. Which city is in a higher place?

　　_____ Chicago _____ Denver

4. Rivers flow from higher land to lower land. Which direction does the Colorado River flow?

　　_____ to the north _____ to the west _____ to the south

5. In which city would you expect to find more stores that sell mountain climbing and ski supplies?

　　_____ San Francisco _____ Denver _____ Dallas

Application:

Use this map to identify the highest land in your area of the country.

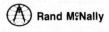

ACTIVITY 6: Using Population Symbols on a U.S. Map

Population means people, and a population density map shows how many people live in a place. This map shows the population density in the United States.

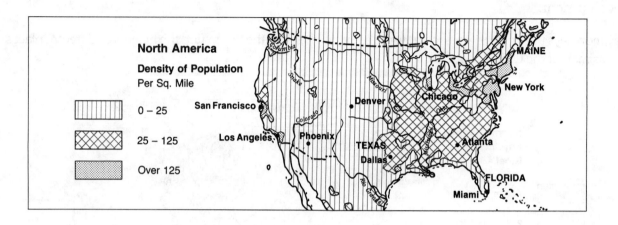

Development: Use the map to answer these questions.

1. What is the symbol for places with 0 - 25 population?

2. What is the symbol for the places with the greatest population density?

3. What is the population density in the area of New York?

_____

4. In which part of the United States do you find more people?

_____ the Northeast _____ the Northwest

5. Which city is in the area of the highest population density?

_____ Denver _____ Chicago

6. Which city is in the area of the lowest population density?

_____ San Franciso _____ Phoenix _____ New York

7. Find this city. It is on a coast in an area that has a population density of 25-125 people per square kilometer. Which city is it?

_____ New York _____ San Francisco _____ Atlanta

Application:

Use this map to find the population density in your part of the country.

Does it have more than one level?

_____

If so, in which area do more people live?

_____

_____

Tell why more people might live there.

_____

_____

_____

Rand McNally

CHAPTER 2: Finding Places

There are many ways to find a place on the earth, and in this section you will learn some of those ways.

ACTIVITY 1: Recognizing Shapes

Development:

Most of the land on the earth is within seven very large land areas called continents. The outlines on this page show the shape of those seven land areas. Use an atlas to match the shapes with the correct continents. Print the name of each continent on the line with the matching letter. It is difficult to see the shape of Antarctica on most maps, but you can see its shape clearly on the map of Antarctica in a polar view.

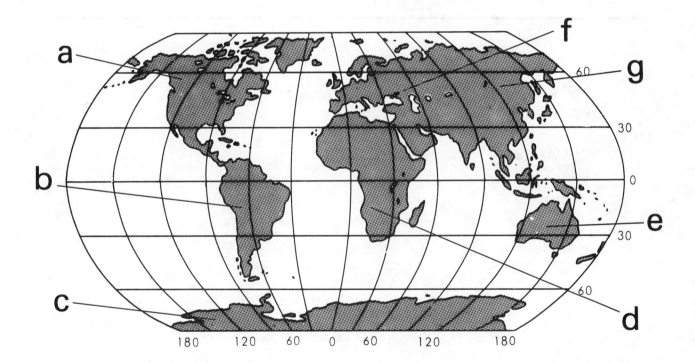

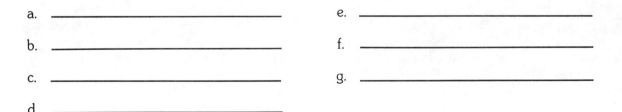

a. _____   e. _____

b. _____   f. _____

c. _____   g. _____

d. _____

ANTARCTICA IN A POLAR VIEW

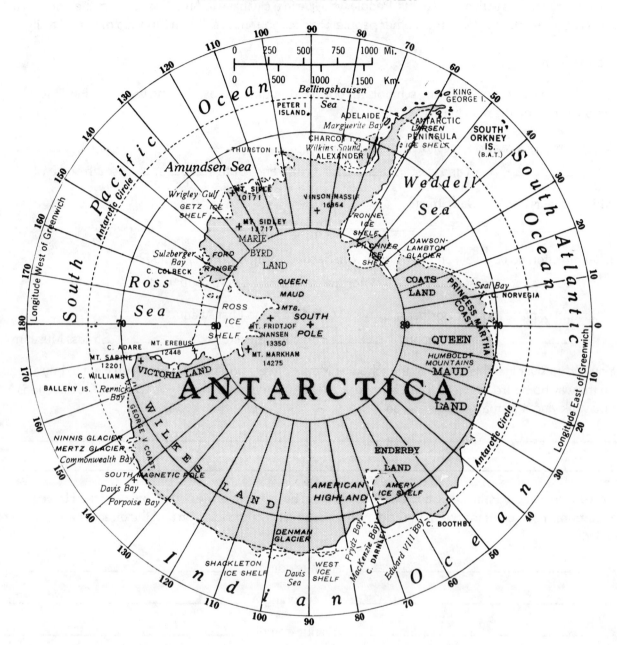

Application:

Every state has a special shape that helps to locate it on a map of the United States. Make a set of outlines of different states. To make your set use a piece of tracing paper. Trace the outline of your own state and of six other states shown on the map of the United States in the atlas. Then set up a chart of those states or make your outline maps into an activity page for another student to label.

ACTIVITY 2: Finding Places in a City

Cities are large places with many streets. People who live in a city have to find the way from their homes to the places they work, shop, and meet other people. Practice your map skills on this map of part of a city.

Development:

Most maps show directions by using symbols for north (N), south (S), east (E), and west (W). Find the direction arrows on the map of River City.

1. Which directions can you travel on Second Avenue?

_____ east and west   _____ north and south   _____ south and east

2. Which street is north of Oak Street?

_____ Elm Street   _____ Palm Drive   _____ First Avenue

3. What direction do you walk on Palm Drive from Second Avenue to First Avenue?

_____ east   _____ northwest   _____ southwest

4. What kind of place is on the northeast corner of Oak Street and First Avenue?

_____ water company   _____ computer store   _____ Strauss Museum

5. You live in River Heights and go to the school at Maple Street and Third Avenue. You want to buy a cake on the way home from school. Tell the route you take, including the streets you walk on, the directions you walk, and how many blocks you go.

_____

_____

6. You get on a bus at Palm Drive and Second Avenue. The bus passes the courthouse and the Harvey Planetarium. You get off the bus at the Zoo. Name the streets you traveled on and the directions in which you traveled.

a. _____ Avenue going _____

b. _____ Street going _____

c. _____ Avenue going _____

d. How far did you travel on the bus? _____ blocks.

Application:

Draw a map that shows the part of your community near your school. Show the different kinds of places on those blocks with symbols. Be sure to include the direction symbols on the map. Then write questions about finding places on that map.

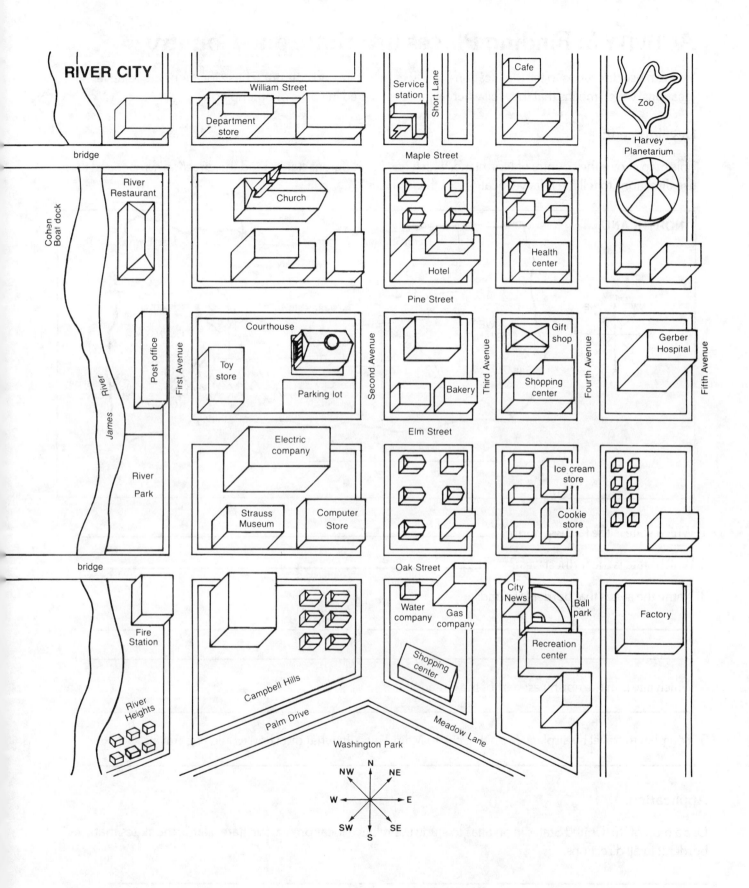

ACTIVITY 3: Finding Places in a State and Country

You can use directions to tell the locations of places in a state and country. Those locations are relative locations, which means that they tell where a place is located in terms of other places.

Development:

This map shows the country of Northland, which has five different states. Find the direction symbol and then use directions to tell the relative locations of these places.

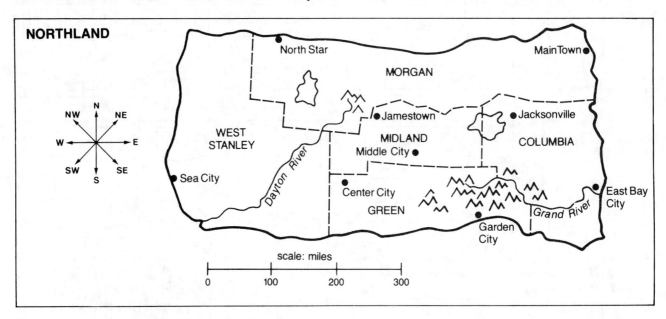

1. Which state is the farthest north? _____

2. Which state is the farthest west? _____

3. Name the states that border Midland.

_____

_____

4. Which city is in the northwest part of the Green State?

_____

5. You plan to travel by airplane from that city to Main Town. In what direction would you travel?

_____

Application:

Use a map of the United States in an atlas to study the relative location of your state. Name the states that border it in all directions.

_____

_____

ACTIVITY 4: Finding Places Using Latitude

North and south are directions on the earth, and they have an important connection with two places, the poles. When you travel north, you are going toward the North Pole, and when you travel south, you are going toward the South Pole. Latitude lines help tell how far north or south you are from the equator.

Development:

Latitude lines are drawn from east to west on maps and globes. The longest latitude line is at the equator, the middle of the earth.

You can see the whole latitude line on a globe, and each one circles the earth. Latitude lines are called parallels of latitudes because they are parallel lines, which means they go in the same direction and are the same distance apart at all points, never touching each other.

Find the latitude of each point in the diagram below. Be sure to mark whether the point is north or south of the equator (0°). Point A is done for you.

1.

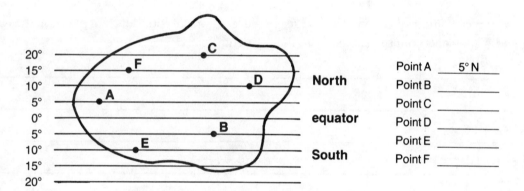

Point A   5° N

Point B _____

Point C _____

Point D _____

Point E _____

Point F _____

Sometimes places on a map are between numbered latitude lines. Then it is necessary to estimate the latitude of a given point. Look at the next diagram. It shows places that are near latitude lines, so you have to estimate their approximate latitude. Point A is done for you. Study it and then do the remaining points.

2.

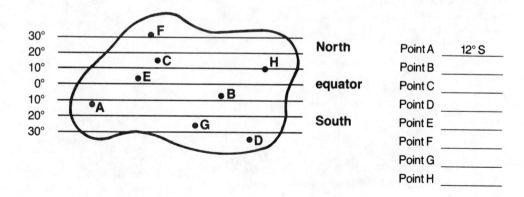

Point A   12° S

Point B _____

Point C _____

Point D _____

Point E _____

Point F _____

Point G _____

Point H _____

Application:

1. Use a globe to trace the equator all the way around the earth. Name the continents it crosses.

   _____

2. On the globe, trace another latitude line. Follow 45° north around the earth. Name the continents it crosses.

   _____

3. Trace a southern latitude line. Follow 30° south around the earth. Name the continents and the oceans that it crosses.

   _____

4. Use an atlas to find important cities in North America at the following latitudes:

   a. Near 40° north in Colorado: _____

   b. At 35° north in Tennessee: _____   and   _____

   c. At 40° north in Pennsylvania: _____

5. Make up your own latitude questions. Write clues to the locations of four different places in the world using latitude. Then give your questions to another student.

   a.   _____

   b.   _____

   c.   _____

   d.   _____

ACTIVITY 5: Finding Places Using Longitude

Longitude lines tell how far east or west a place is located. You will find these lines on maps and globes. Together with latitude lines, they make a set of lines called a grid that people use to locate places on the earth.

Development:

Lines of longitude, or meridians of longitude, are drawn from north to south. The numbers on these lines tell how far east or west they are of the prime meridian. The prime meridian is a longitude line that runs through Greenwich, England, near London. You can follow a longitude line from the North Pole to the South Pole. The longitude lines meet at the two poles.

Find the longitude of each point in this diagram. Be sure to mark whether each point is east or west of the Prime Meridian. Point A is done for you.

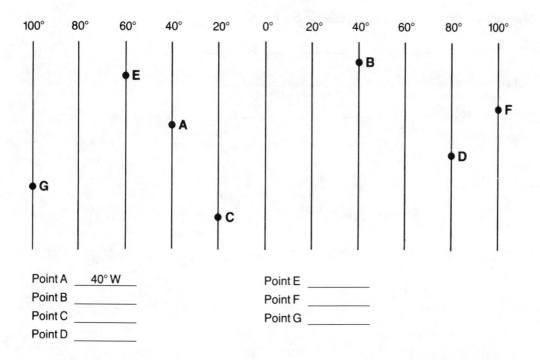

Point A ___40° W___   Point E _____

Point B _____   Point F _____

Point C _____   Point G _____

Point D _____

Application:

(This activity requires the use of a globe.)

1. On a globe, find the prime meridian, which is labelled 0°. Name the continent that it crosses to the south of Europe.

   _____

2. Find the place that is at 0°, 0°. It is at the prime meridian and at the equator. Where are you when you are at 0°, 0°?

   _____

Ⓐ **Rand McNally**

3. How far west do the United States extend? To find out, look for the Hawaiian Islands at about 25° north and for the westernmost part of the state of Alaska. At about what degree of longitude west are those places?

_____West

4. Find 180° of longitude. It is the point where east meets west. Follow it from the south pole to the north pole. What land areas does it cross?

_____

5. Use the globe to locate important cities in North America at the following longitudes:

a. 90° west in Louisiana _____

b. about 100° west in Mexico _____

6. Use the globe to locate places at the following longitudes in South America.

a. The mouth of this river is at 50° west in Brazil: _____

b. This city is along that same river at 60° west: _____

c. These islands are very far south at 60° west: _____

ACTIVITY 6: Using Time Zones

Knowing longitude helps you tell time anywhere on the earth. People use longitude to divide the world into 24 time zones.

Development:

The longitude line at 180° is very important because it is the International Date Line. This line is one-half of the way around the world from 0 degrees longitude. Time changes a day when you cross this line. A person traveling west across this line adds a day. So if a plane leaves Samoa (about 170° west) on Monday and flies west to Fiji, which is on the west side of the International Date Line, when that plane lands in Fiji it will be Tuesday, not Monday. Then, flying back, if the plane left Fiji on Tuesday, the passengers would gain a day. When they reached Samoa, it would be Monday.

The following diagram shows the time zones and the International Date Line. Study the diagram and then answer the questions about time zones.

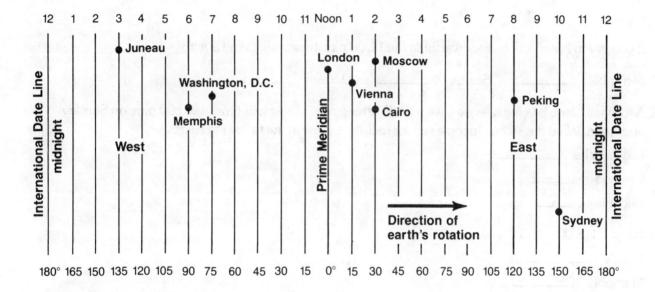

1. What time is shown in each city:

   Memphis _____   Sydney _____

   Cairo _____   Washington, D.C. _____

   Peking _____   London _____

   Juneau _____   Moscow _____

2. Compute the difference in hours between each pair of cities:

   a. Memphis and London _____   d. Sydney and Washington, D.C. _____

   b. Peking and Moscow _____   e. Memphis and Washington, D.C. _____

   c. Cairo and Peking _____

Rand McNally

This diagram shows the time zones in the United States. Use it to answer the following questions.

TIME ZONES, IN THE UNITED STATES

3. If you live in New York and are watching the 11:00 p.m. news, what time is it in:

   Memphis _____   Seattle _____   Denver _____

4. A football game is being televised live from Washington, D.C. At half-time, it is 3:00 p.m. on Sunday afternoon. What time would people see the half-time show in the following cities:

   Los Angeles _____

   Chicago _____

   Phoenix _____

5. When it is 8:00 a.m. in Denver, what time is it in:

   Seattle _____

   Memphis _____

   Chicago _____

   Salt Lake City _____

Application:

Make a chart of the time in different parts of the United States when it is 9:00 a.m. in your community and when it is 9:00 p.m.

ACTIVITY 7: Finding Places Using the Latitude-Longitude Grid

Latitude and longitude lines help people locate places anywhere on the earth.

Development:

This drawing shows a latitude and longitude grid for an imaginary place.

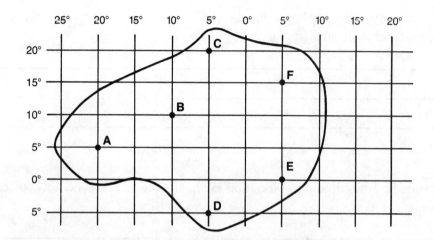

Write the letter of the point described by each pair of latitude-longitude locations.

1. 5°N, 20°W _____
2. 15°N, 5°E _____
3. 0°, 5°E _____

4. 5°S, 5°W _____
5. 10°N, 10°W _____
6. 20°N, 5°W _____

Application:

Use a globe to find the cities that are at or near the following exact locations in the world.

1. 30°N, 90°W: _____

2. 60°N, 15°E: _____

3. 0°, 105°E: _____

Tell the exact location using latitude and longitude of your own community. Use the globe to find the closest lines of latitude and longitude to your location in North America.

_____ N, _____ W

ACTIVITY 8: Explaining Location

Now it is your turn to explain how to find places in the world. In your own words explain how people can use map skills to find one place in the world: your own community. You are writing to tell visitors from London, England, how to get to your community. First they have to cross the Atlantic Ocean. What do they do next?

Finish these paragraphs.

1. Using Directions:

To get to my community, you need to know directions. Once you reach North America, you can use directions to find my community in this way.

_____

_____

_____

2. Using Latitude:

Latitude will help you find my community, too. This is what latitude means and how you can use it to find my community:

_____

_____

_____

3. Using Longitude:

Longitude will help you get here, too. You are starting from a place that is near 0° longitude. My community is west of yours. Longitude will help you find how far west it is. Here is some longitude information you will need to use to find me.

_____

_____

_____

_____

CHAPTER 3: Measuring Distances

The earth is 24,901.46 miles around at the equator, and that is the longest distance you could travel if you went around the world once. There are many places to visit, and it is important to know how far you would travel to get there. In this section, you will learn how to find how far it is from one place to another.

ACTIVITY 1: Using a Map Scale

The space on a map is much smaller than the place the map shows, but people can use a map to find distances between real places. People use a scale to find distances with a map.

Development:

A map scale shows how space on a map equals distance on the earth. You can use a map scale to find how far apart places are. To find the distance between Bergen and Oslo in Norway, follow these steps.

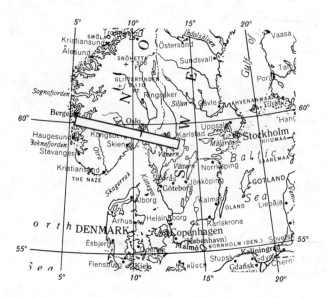

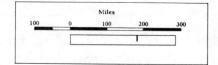

1. Find Bergen and Oslo on the map.

2. Lay a slip of paper on the map so that its edge makes a line between the two cities.

3. Put two marks on the edge of the paper, one where it touches Bergen and one where it touches Oslo.

4. Place the paper along the scale of miles for this map. Match the first mark with the 0 on that line. Then check how far away in miles the other mark is. That mark shows that Bergen is about 200 miles from Oslo.

   Use the map scale to find out how far Bergen is from these cities:

   a. Stavanger _____ miles; b. Stockholm _____ miles;

   c. Copenhagen: _____ miles

Application:

Use a map from an atlas to figure distances between cities in your state.

ACTIVITY 2: Using a Highway Map Scale

When people plan a trip, they need to know how far apart places are, so they use a highway map and a map scale.

Development:

Use this highway map and the scale to figure how far a family traveled on a trip.

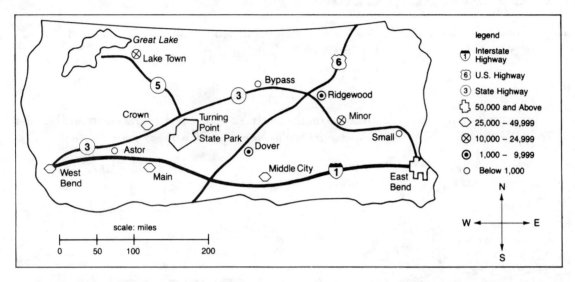

1. The family started at East Bend. They drove west from East Bend for 200 miles on Interstate Highway 1. What city did they visit at that point?

   _____

2. The family drove all the way to West Bend the next day.
   How many miles did they drive in that one day? _____

3. Where did this family stop on its way from West Bend to the Great Lake on State Highway 3:

   a. 150 miles east of West Bend they visited the town of _____

   b. 50 miles east of that city: _____

   c. They drove 100 miles northwest and stopped at: _____

   d. How many more miles did they drive to the Great Lake? _____

   e. They wanted to take the shortest route back to East Bend from the lake. They drove to Turning Point State Park, then all the way to East Bend on Highway 3.
      How many miles was that trip? _____

   How much shorter was it than their first trip? _____

Application:

Use a map of the United States in an Atlas to find out how far it is from: Washington, D.C., to Boston, Massachusetts; Miami, Florida, to Atlanta, Georgia; Los Angeles, California, to Dallas, Texas. Which trip would be the longest? _____

ACTIVITY 3: Contrasting Distances

When people build railroads, they try to make them as straight as possible so trains will travel as quickly as possible. Sometimes the trains have to go around mountains or lakes. Airplanes can fly across mountains and lakes, so they can go more directly. In this activity, you will contrast the distances of trains and planes traveling between the same places.

Development:

Use the scale on the map of Northland to answer the questions that follow.

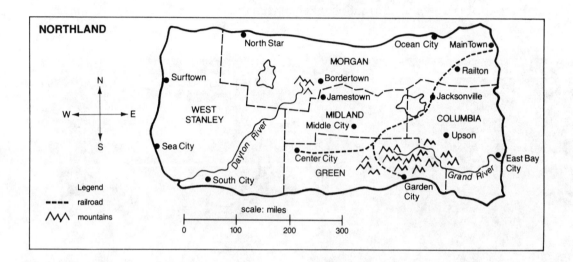

1. How far does a plane fly from Garden City to Main Town?   _____

2. Follow the train route from Garden City to Main Town.

   How many miles does the train travel?   _____

3. If the train did not have to go around the mountains in the state of Green, but could go directly to the northeast from Garden City to Main Town, about how much shorter would that trip be? _____ miles

4. The country of Northland is an island. A cruise line offers a special summer tour by ship. The ship leaves Maintown and travels south. It docks near Garden City. How far has the ship traveled? (To find out, you could use a string to trace the ship's trip and then use that string and the scale to find the miles.) _____ miles

Application:

Plan a new railroad line or highway in your state. Use a state map to find the places you want to connect with this road. Then figure out how long the road will be.

ACTIVITY 4: Tracing Explorers' Routes

When explorers traveled in new places, they made maps to show where they had been. If they could keep track of the miles they traveled, other people could follow their routes. In 1803, President Thomas Jefferson sent Meriwether Lewis and William Clark to look for a river route from the Mississippi River to the northwest coast of North America. First they traveled to St. Louis. Then in spring, they traveled through unmapped areas. In this activity you will follow their route and read some of their reports.

Development:

This report describes the trip of Lewis and Clark. It includes some notes they made on their journey. Add more facts to the report. Fill in the blanks with information you get from the map.

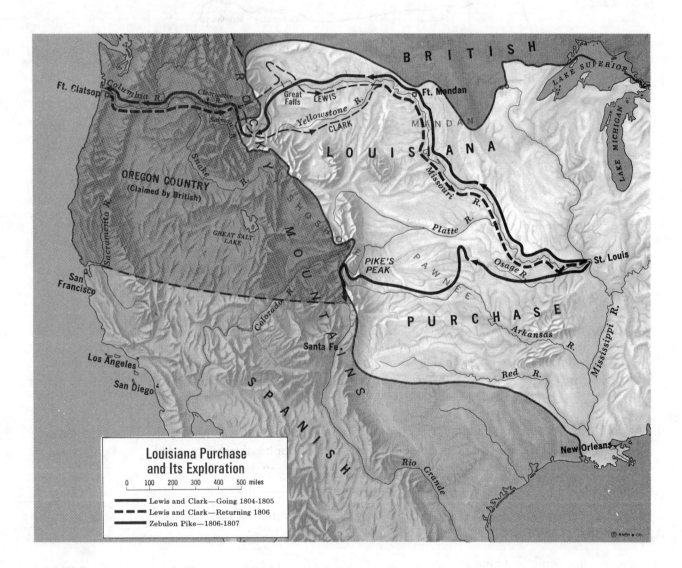

1. The group started from St. Louis on May 14, 1804. About _____ miles from St. Louis they came to the mouth of the Osage River.

2. For about _____ more miles, they traveled mostly to the west. Then the river turned to the northwest. It also became very rapid. On May 24, Clark wrote, 'The swiftness of the current turned the boat, broke our tow rope, and was nearly overturning the boat; all hands jumped out....'

3. The group camped near the place where the Platte River joins the Missouri River. That night Clark wrote in his report that they had traveled _____ miles from St. Louis. He didn't know how much longer they would have to travel to reach the ocean. It would take many days.

4. On October 29, Lewis and Clark met with the chief of the Mandan nation. Then they built Fort Mandan as their winter camp. On April 7, the group sent a boat back to St. Louis with reports. How far did that boat have to travel? _____

5. Lewis and Clark set out again from Fort Mandan. On April 25, Lewis wrote, "The water froze on the oars this morning as the men rowed." They camped that night near the mouth of the Yellowstone River. How far had they come from Fort Mandan? _____ miles

6. From June 21 to July 15, they camped at Great Falls. How fast did they travel between the Yellowstone River and Great Falls? _____ (To find out, divide the number of miles they traveled by the number of days.)

7. On July 28 they set out to the west, where Sacajawea, a Shoshone woman in the group, met her brother, who was a chief. Lewis wrote, "I asked the chief to instruct me in the geography of his country. He did this cheerfully, drawing the rivers on the ground." With that help, they found their way across the Rocky Mountains. On September 29, they reached the Clearwater River and made canoes. How far were they from the Pacific Ocean? _____

8. On November 19, they reached the coast. In the spring, they started back, to St. Louis. How far did they have to travel? _____

Application:

Use a map of any place in the world that you would like to have explored. Trace your route. Write a report about that place as if you were the first person to visit it.

Ⓐ Rand McNally

ACTIVITY 5: Crossing the United States

In this activity you will follow one group of people across the country in 1849. They are going to California where they hope to find gold.

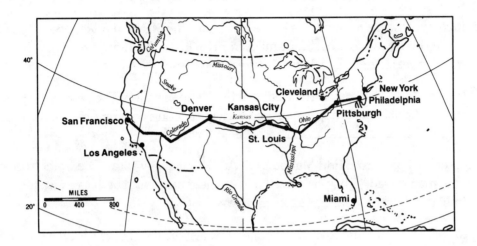

Development:

Use the map scale to answer these questions.

1. The group starts at Philadelphia. They travel by train west to Pittsburgh.
   They have traveled _____ miles.

2. They travel _____ miles west from Pittsburgh by river boat on the Ohio and Mississippi Rivers to St. Louis.

3. They travel west along the river to Kansas City. The trip from St. Louis to Kansas City is _____ miles.

4. At Kansas City, they start west by land. They travel about 600 miles west to the city of _____. They decide to stay there because they do not want to to cross the Rocky Mountains.

5. That trip took months. Today people can fly from Philadelphia to San Francisco in hours. How far do they travel by air? _____ miles

Application:

Make up a set of clues for finding different cities in the United States. Here is an example.

You start in New York City. You go straight west about 420 miles to a city on a large lake. Where are you? (You are in Cleveland.)

Use the map on this page or maps in the atlas to choose cities and figure how far apart they are.

CHAPTER 4: Profiling Places

Maps show many different things about a place, and they can show how places change. In this section you will learn how to use different maps to tell many things about the same place.

ACTIVITY 1: Using Maps to Choose Locations

The map on this page shows the land in an imaginary place. People can use maps like it to make choices about where to live and about how to use the land in a place.

Development:

Use this map to answer the questions that follow.

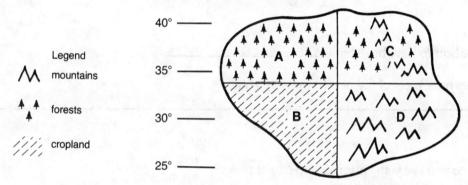

WILDERNESS AREA MAP

1. Cindy wants to build her house in Section D. Decide whether this is a good choice and give your reasons.

_____

_____

2. In which section would Terri want to buy land to start a farm?

_____

3. Contrast section C with Section B.

_____

_____

4. In which area of Wilderness would you most like to live?   Why?

_____

Application:

Make your own map of an imaginary place. Then make your own set of questions about locations in that place. Share your project with other members of your class.

ACTIVITY 2: Contrasting Maps

Look back at the map of River City on page 23. That map shows the city after many changes have taken place. The map on this page shows River City 20 years earlier, before those changes. Contrast the maps. Then answer the questions.

Contrast the two maps of River City and then complete this chart.

Stores:

What new stores have opened?

What stores have closed?

Homes:

How many new homes have been built? _____

On which streets have most of the new homes been built?

Parks:

What changes do you see in the number and size of parks?

Other Changes:

What else do you notice that is different between River City as it was 20 years ago and as it is shown today in the maps?

Application:

Plan more changes for River City. Make a map of your own showing how you would make it a better city ten years from today.

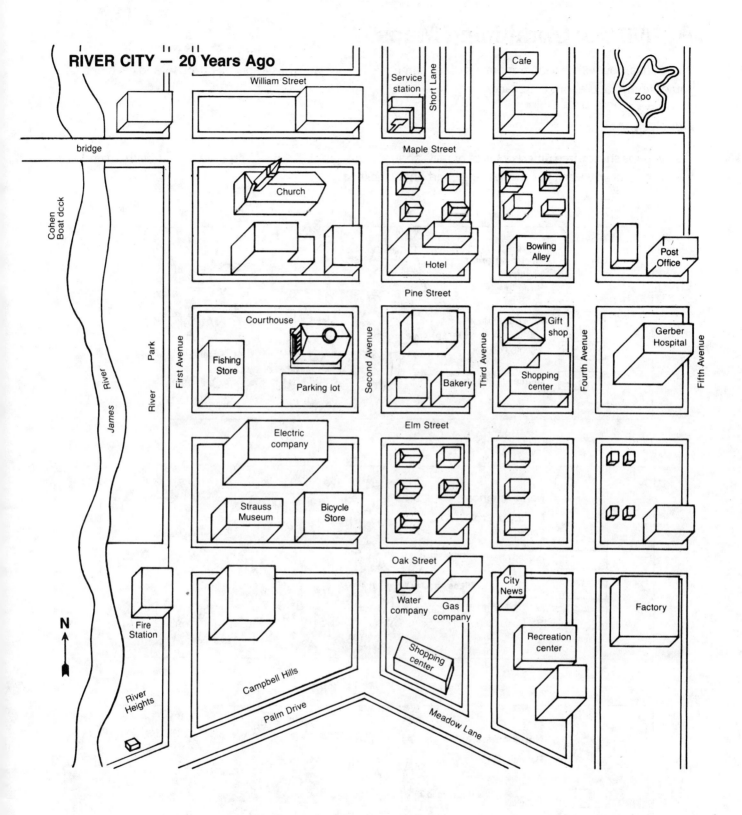

RIVER CITY — 20 Years Ago

William Street

Service station

Short Lane

Cafe

Zoo

bridge

Maple Street

Cohen Boat dcck

Church

Hotel

Bowling Alley

Post Office

Pine Street

James River

River Park

First Avenue

Courthouse

Fishing Store

Parking lot

Second Avenue

Bakery

Third Avenue

Gift shop

Shopping center

Fourth Avenue

Gerber Hospital

Fifth Avenue

Elm Street

Electric company

Strauss Museum

Bicycle Store

N

Fire Station

Oak Street

Water company

Gas company

City News

Recreation center

Factory

Shopping center

River Heights

Campbell Hills

Palm Drive

Meadow Lane

ACTIVITY 3: Combining Maps

In the atlas, you will find different maps of the same place. Each map has a special purpose, and each one tells you different facts about that place.

Development:

These maps show three different kinds of facts about the geography of the United States. Study them and then use what you learn to complete the chart on the next page.

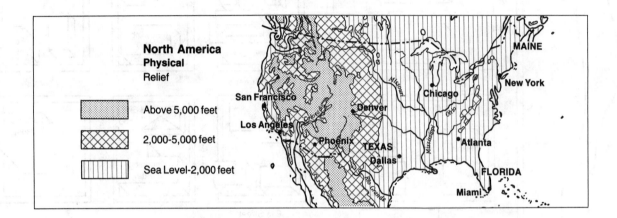

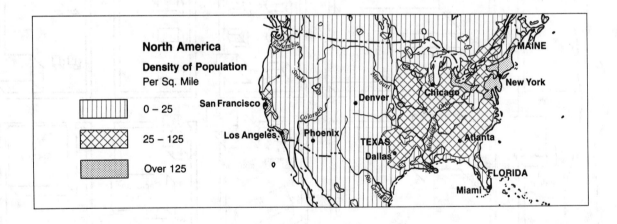

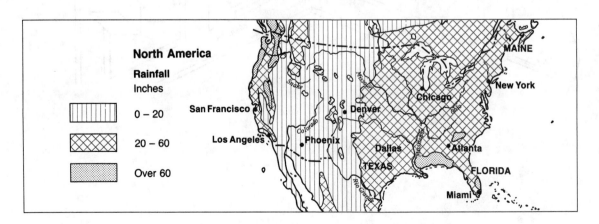

Find these three states on the three maps. Then make notes on the chart about the kind of rainfall, land, and population you find in each state.

	FLORIDA	TEXAS	MAINE
how much rainfall			
how high the land is there			
where in the state most people live			

Use your chart and the maps to describe these features.

1. Rainfall in Florida. _____

2. Relief in Maine. _____

3. Population in Texas. _____

4. A farmer wants to buy land in a state that has much rainfall and no mountains. In which of the three states would a farmer be most likely to find what he wants? _____

5. Use the population map to answer this question. In which parts of the United States do most people live?

_____

6. Look for those places on the elevation map. What connection do you see between how high the land is and where the people live?

_____

Application:

Write a description of one state's land, rainfall, and population. You could write about one of the three states in your chart or any other state you locate on the three maps.

ACTIVITY 4: Choosing a Map to Use

People use different maps for different reasons. In this activity you will learn to choose the correct type of map to learn about a place.

Development:

Look closely at both maps. Find Chicago in the map on the right.

The first map is a map of Chicago, Illinois. You will see highways within the city. However, if we wanted to show a larger area, the highways would disappear from the city, and Chicago would appear much smaller in order to show more information on the map. The second map shows the area surrounding Lake Michigan.

1. On which map can you find more information about Chicago?

   _____

2. What information is shown on the second map that the first map does not show?

   _____

3. Why might a person use the first map rather than the second?

   _____

4. Why might a person use the second map rather than the first?

   _____

MAP 1: CHICAGO, ILLINOIS

MAP 2: CITIES NEAR SOUTHWEST LAKE MICHIGAN

Application:

Look for Chicago on maps of the United States on page 42. Then contrast those maps with the two on page 44.

1. What facts do the maps of the United States provide about Chicago that these two maps do not give?

_____

_____

2. Why might you use them instead of one of these two maps?

_____

_____

3. What information would you put on a map to show how to find places in your community?

_____

_____

_____

_____

ACTIVITY 5: Creating A Map—A Special Project

In this activity, you will use your map skills to make maps. Most map makers show places that are really part of the world, but in this activity you will show an imaginary place. Your map should show a place that could be part of the world.

ROUNDLAND

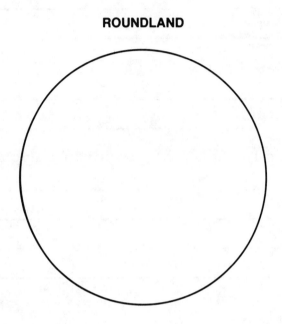

1. Draw a compass rose next to the map. Show north, south, east, west, and northeast, northwest, southeast, southwest.

2. Draw a legend or key for the map. Make symbols for: the capital city, farmland, forests, mountains and plains.

3. Use your symbol for forests to put one in the northwest section of Roundland.

4. Use your symbol for farmland to show farming in the southeast.

5. Draw in at least one river. Remember that rivers flow from higher land to lower land. Show the mountains and have your river start in the mountains and move to the sea.

6. Make at least one other map of Roundland. Show a special feature of this country, such as rainfall.

7. Write a brief tour guide to Roundland pointing out the important places to visit. Your tour guide can include pictures you draw of what people might see if they really visited such a place.

ROUNDLAND

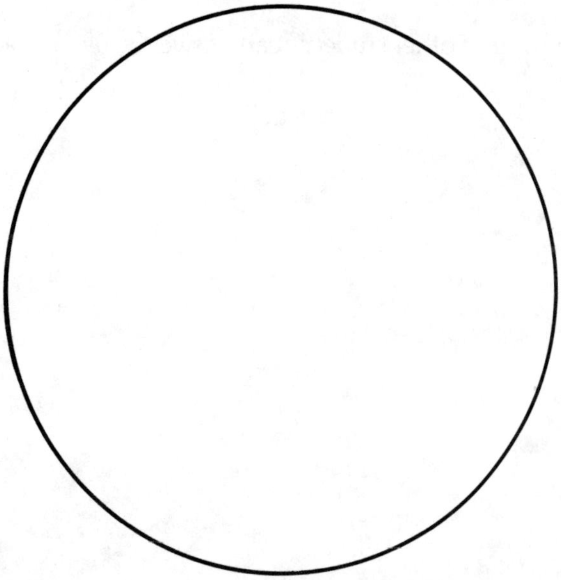

_____

_____

_____

_____

_____

_____

_____

_____

Create a map of another country, Pineland. Start by making the title, scale, legend, and compass rose. Include these items on your map: a coastline on the ocean, forests, plains, hills, a capital city, other cities, various crops, highways, railroad lines.

After you finish write five questions that other students can answer by using your map.

Questions about Pineland

1. _____

   _____

2. _____

   _____

3. _____

   _____

4. _____

   _____

5. _____

   _____

CHAPTER 5: Using the Atlas

Note to students: The atlas holds the whole world in maps. Once you have the skills to read maps, you can find any place on earth and know what you would see if you visited that place. You will learn these skills in this part of the workbook. Start here to learn how to use the atlas to explore any place on the earth. First get an atlas, then start to explore.

ACTIVITY 1: Looking for Facts

Every atlas holds key facts about the world. This list from the Classroom Atlas tells some surprising facts about the world.

WORLD FACTS AND COMPARISONS

Movements of the Earth

The earth makes one complete revolution around the sun every 365 days, 5 hours, 48 minutes, and 46 seconds. It requires 23 hours and 56 minutes to make one complete rotation on its axis. The earth revolves in its orbit around the sun at a speed of 66,700 miles per hour, and rotates on its axis at an equatorial speed of more than 1,000 miles per hour.

The Earth's Inhabitants

Total population of the earth is estimated to be 4,883,000,000 (January 1, 1986). Its estimated population density is 84 per square mile.

The Earth's Surface

Highest point on the earth's surface: Mount Everest, China—Nepal, 29,028 feet.
Lowest point on the earth's land surface: shores of the Dead Sea, Israel-Jordan, 1,312 feet below sea level (1982).
Greatest ocean depth: the Marianas Trench, south of Guam, Pacific Ocean, 35,810 feet.

Measurements of the Earth

Estimated age: at least 3 billion years.
Equatorial diameter: 7,926.68 miles.
Polar diameter: 7,899.99 miles.

Mean diameter: 7,918.78 miles.
Equatorial circumference: 24,901.46 miles.
Polar circumference: 24,859.73 miles.
Difference between equatorial and polar circumference: 41.73 miles.
Weight: 6.6 sextillion or 6,600 billion billion tons.
Total area: 196,940,400 square miles.
Total land area (including inland water and Antarctica); 57,800,000 square miles.

Temperature and Rainfall Extremes

Highest temperature ever recorded: 136.4°F. at Al 'Azīzīyah, Libya, Africa, on September 13, 1922.
Lowest temperature ever recorded: −126.9°F. at Vostok, Antarctica, on August 24, 1960.
Highest mean annual temperature: 88°F. at Lugh Ferrandi, Somalia.
Lowest mean annual temperature: −67°F. at Vostok, Antarctica.
At Cilaos, Reunion Island, in the Indian Ocean, 74 inches of rainfall was reported in a 24-hour period, March 15-16, 1952. This is believed to be the world's record for a 24-hour rainfall.
An authenticated rainfall of 366 inches in 1 month—July, 1861—was reported at Cherrapunji, India. More than 131 inches fell in a period of 7 consecutive days in June, 1931. Average annual rainfall at Cherrapunji is 450 inches.

Development:

Answer these questions by reading the list carefully.

1. Where is the lowest land on the earth? _____

2. What is the estimated age of the earth _____ (how old do people think it is)?

3. Where on the earth was it − 126.9 degrees Farenheit on August 24, 1960? _____

4. How fast does the earth travel on its orbit around the sun? _____

Application:

Now that you have found the answers write four more questions using these facts and other facts you find in the atlas.

ACTIVITY 2: Finding Maps with the Table of Contents

Some maps show all the cities and towns in a state, while some other maps show different kinds of facts about a place. When you use the atlas, you need to know the different kinds of maps. Use an atlas to answer the following questions.

Development:

Here are two kinds of maps you will find in an atlas:

Political Maps: These maps use lines, dots, and other symbols to show the countries, states, and cities in the world. A political map can show a small area or the whole world.

Find a political map in the atlas that shows the United States. To find that map, use the Table of Contents in the front of the atlas. Use that map to answer these questions.

1. On what page in the atlas is the political map of the United States? _____

2. Find your state on the map on that page. Then look to see which states border your state. Write their names. _____

   Find a political map that shows the whole world. To find it, use the Table of Contents again.

3. On what page is this map of the world? _____

4. Find the United States on this map. Then write the names of four other countries that share the continent of North America with the United States.

   _____

Special Purpose Maps: These maps show special features of a place. They can show how much rain falls in a place, how many people live there, and what kinds of crops grow there. Look through the Table of Contents to find a special purpose map. Then look at the maps themselves to find one that tells you more about the United States.

5. What is the title of the map you chose? _____

6. Write one fact it shows about this country.

   _____

Application:

Choose one state in the United States. Find it on the maps of North America, the United States maps, and on at least one regional map. Make a list of the maps in the atlas you could use to learn about that state. Then start a fact sheet for that state. You will add more facts as you learn more about using the atlas.

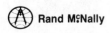 **Rand McNally**

Activity 3: Using Color Symbols

Every map uses symbols to show places. Some maps only use lines, but many maps use color to show where things are located. You need to use the legend or key for that map to find what the color symbols stand for. Use an atlas to answer the following questions.

Development:

Use the Table of Contents to find the map in the atlas that shows the natural vegetation of the world. It shows the kind of vegetation, or plants that you would find in the different places on the earth. Use that map to answer these questions.

1. What color does the map use to show that there is little or no vegetation in a place?

_____

2. Which continent has little or no vegetation on most of its land?

_____

3. What color does the map use to show desert grass or shrub?

_____

4. Name the continents on which you find desert lands.

_____

5. If you visited the northernmost part of North America, what kind of vegetation would you see there?

_____

Application:

Study the map in the atlas that shows North American vegetation. Use the key and the cities located on that map to answer these questions.

6. Choose one city and describe the vegetation in its area.

   a. the city: _____

   b. the kind of vegetation there: _____

7. Look for your state on the map. What kind of vegetation does the map show for your part of North America?

_____

ACTIVITY 4: Finding Places with the Index

Long ago people guessed where places were, and sometimes they made very great mistakes. Today you can use maps to find any place you want to explore. Use an atlas index to answer the following questions.

Development:

The atlas index lists places in alphabetical order and tells the page number of the map that shows each place. It also tells where to look on the map. Here is an example of how it works.

A. You start by looking for the place-name. Look for Chicago, Illinois.

Cherbourg, Fr.	F7	63
Cherkassy, Sov. Un.	F14	63
Chernigov, Sov. Un.	E14	63
Chernovtsy, Sov. Un.	E5	71
Chetumal, Mex.	H12	27
Cheyenne, Wy.	B6	39
Chiang Rai, Thai.	H12	71
Chicago, Il.	B9	39
Chiclayo, Peru	D3	55
Chicoutimi, P.Q.	G19	35
Chihuahua, Mex.	G10	27
Chile, S.A.	G3	55

B. The Index shows that Chicago is on the map on what page? _____
   The letter-number guide (B9) will help you to find Chicago on that map.

C. Turn to the page in your atlas that shows Chicago on a political map.

D. Look for the letter-number guide. Find the letters A through F and the numbers 1 through 13 along the sides of the map.

E. Place your left hand index finger on the letter B at the left side of the map and your right index finger on the number 9 at the bottom of the map.

F. Move your left pointer finger to the right, and move your right pointer finger toward the top of the map. Your fingers should meet at Chicago.

Now you are ready to find more places. Use the Index to find each of these places. First, look for the map that shows the location of each place. Then use the maps to complete the sentences about each place.

1. Mexico City, Mexico, is shown on the map on page _____.

2. Nairobi is the capital city of the country of _____.

3. Manaus is a city in _____.

   Manaus is near a large river there called the _____.

4. Genoa is a city in _____. It is on the coast of the _____ Sea.

Application:

Name a place you would like to visit. Then use the Index to find its location on a map. Use that map and other maps in the atlas to find facts about that place and nearby places. Start a list of those facts and keep adding to it as you learn more map skills.

 **Rand McNally**

ACTIVITY 5: Your Place in the Atlas—A Special Project

The atlas shows many facts about many places in the world. Each place is different, and each one is special. If the atlas showed all the facts about every place on the earth, it would be millions of pages long. It can not be that long, so it does not show every fact about every place. You can add some facts about your community to the atlas. In each section of this map skills unit, you will learn about geography. Start to make a special section for the atlas now and keep adding to your section as you learn more about maps and geography.

Begin by listing facts you know about your community. Use this outline to make your lists.

1. Important places in my community

_____

_____

2. My state

_____

_____

3. Important places in my state

_____

_____

Add more facts about your part of the United States. To get those facts, find your state on the maps of the United States and of North America in the atlas. Use this outline to guide you as you collect facts from those maps.

A. Kinds of vegetation in this part of the United States

_____

_____

B. Important cities in this part of the United States

_____

_____

C. Large rivers, lakes, or other bodies of water in or near my community

_____

_____

Geographers learn about places by visiting them and by getting reports from people who live in those places. Write a short report for a geographer who lives far away from your community. In your report tell about the usual kind of weather in your community. Describe the kind of land in the area.

Part Two /
Developing Skills with Graphs

A graph is a special tool used to show facts. You can use a graph to show the population of penguins in Antarctica or the number of pickles in a grocery store. To show facts in a graph, you use symbols. Some graphs use pictures, others use bars, lines, or circles. Whatever symbol you see on a graph, remember that it stands for how much or how many. In Part 2, you will use graphs to keep track of rain, snow, fish, peanuts, and ice cream cones. Then, when it's your turn, you can use graphs to keep track of anything in the world.

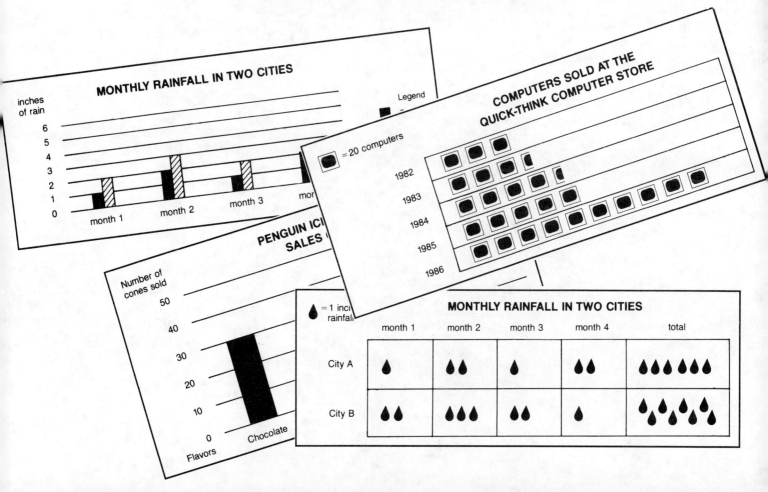

CHAPTER 1: Using Picture Graphs

Picture graphs use symbols to stand for numbers of things. A picture of a car can stand for that one car, but in a picture graph it also can stand for hundreds or thousands of cars. Picture graphs can help show the number of cars, trucks, computers, or other things represented.

ACTIVITY 1: Getting Facts from a Picture Graph

Development:

A picture graph shows facts that you can find by using the pictures, and the key tells what those pictures represent.

💧 = 1 inch rainfall

MONTHLY RAINFALL IN TWO CITIES

	month 1	month 2	month 3	month 4	total
City A	💧	💧💧	💧	💧💧	💧💧💧💧💧💧
City B	💧💧	💧💧💧	💧💧	💧	💧💧💧💧💧💧💧💧

This picture graph shows how many inches of rain fell in two cities over a four-month period. Each raindrop symbol equals one inch of rain. It is easy to see that City B had more rain than City A.

1. How many total inches of rain did City A receive? _____

   What is the total inches of rain for City B? _____

2. In which month did City B get the most rain? _____

3. In which month did City A get more rain than City B? _____

4. Which city got more rain in Month 3? _____

5. How much rain did both cities get altogether in Month 4? _____

Application:

Get the weather report for your community and add up the rain or snow that falls for four weeks. Then make a picture graph like this one for your own community. If there is no rainfall, then you can make a picture graph that shows other weather facts, such as the number of sunny days, cloudy days, or hot and cold days.

 Rand McNally

ACTIVITY 2: Interpreting a Picture Graph

Once you know how to find the facts in a picture graph, you are ready to do much more. The facts you find are starting points. It is up to you to figure out, or interpret, what those facts tell about a topic. In this activity you will learn how to interpret information from picture graphs.

Development:

The picture graph below shows students in six different classes.

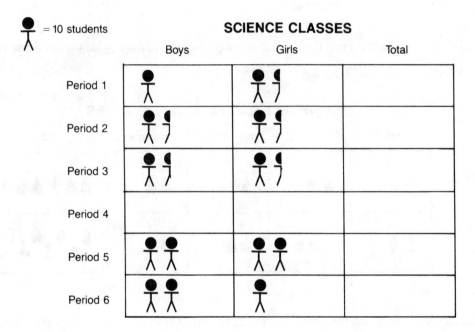

First fill in the <u>Total column</u>. Use picture symbols to show the total number of students in each class. Then use the graph to answer the questions.

True - False: Write T for statements that are true and F for those that are false.

1. _____ There are more girls than boys in all the science classes.

2. _____ The total number of science students is 155.

3. _____ The largest science class is in period 1.

4. _____ There are 75 boys in all the science classes.

5. _____ The classroom has 30 microscopes, so there always are enough microscopes for every student to have one.

Application:

Make a picture graph like this one for your own school. You could show the number of students in different classrooms at the same grade level, in different subjects, or in different grades. Then write your own true-false questions about the graph you make.

ACTIVITY 3: Summarizing a Picture Graph

This graph shows the number of computers that were sold by a computer store during a five-year time period. You will use it to summarize these facts.

Development:

Study this graph to find information about the computers the store sold. Then answer the questions that follow.

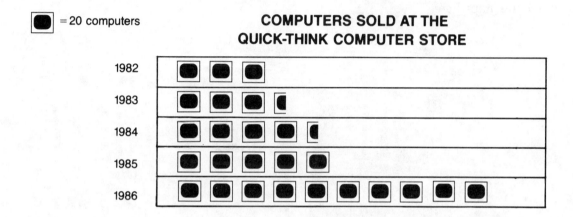

= 20 computers

COMPUTERS SOLD AT THE QUICK-THINK COMPUTER STORE

1. What does the graph show about the sales of computers in five years?

   _____ Every year sales increased.   _____ One year sales decreased.

   _____ The best year for sales was 1984.   _____ The store sold 400 computers.

2. One year the store sold twice as many computers as the year before. Which year was that?

   _____ 1983   _____ 1984   _____ 1985   _____ 1986

3. The store owner plans to sell computers in 1987. How many computers do you think the store might sell, if it sells as many as it sold in 1986?

   _____ 100   _____ 120   _____ 80   _____ 200

4. The store owner is thinking of opening another store in another part of town. What information in this graph makes that seem like a good idea?

   _____ People bought many computers in 1986.

   _____ People are using computers in more businesses.

   _____ People are buying more and more computers, because they are cheaper.

   _____ People are using computers in schools.

Application:

Draw a picture graph to show the favorite foods of your classmates. Then summarize what that graph tells about your class.

ACTIVITY 4: Do It Yourself—A Special Project

Now it is your turn. Choose a topic you like and show some number facts about that topic in a picture graph. You could show the different kinds of fruits, vegetables, meats, and other foods you eat in a week. Or you could show something imaginary, such as the different kinds of clothes a store sells in a day. The important thing to remember in making a picture graph is that the pictures are symbols. Each one stands for a number of one kind of thing. If each picture stands for just one thing, then you don't need to explain how many each one represents. To make a picture graph like the computer graph in which one picture stands for more than one computer, you have to make a key to show how many each picture represents.

Draw your picture graph here.

Make a key. Then write five questions about the facts your graph shows.

1. _____

2. _____

3. _____

4. _____

5. _____

CHAPTER 2: Bar Graphs

Bar graphs can show the same kind of information as picture graphs. It is easier to draw bars than pictures; and sometimes a bar graph shows information in a way that makes it easier to compare and contrast.

ACTIVITY 1: Getting Facts from a Bar Graph

This bar graph shows how much rain fell in two different places. The numbers along the left side of the graph show how much rain each section of the bars represents.

Development:

This graph shows the same information as the picture graph on page 57. It uses a different kind of bar to show each city.

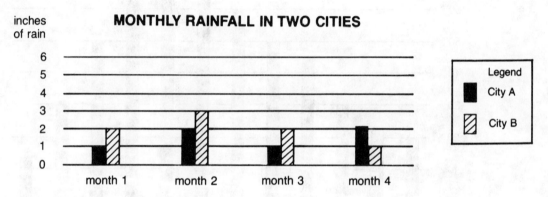

1. Which city is shown by the solid bar? _____

2. Which city is shown by the striped bar? _____

3. Which city received more rain in Month 1? _____

4. How much rain did City B receive in Month 3? _____

5. How much more rain fell in City B than City A in Month 2? _____

6. What is the total amount of rain for the four months in City A? _____

7. What is the total amount of rain for the four months in City B. _____

8. Which city received more rain during the four months? _____

Application:

Make a bar graph for the temperatures in your community for four weeks. First make a framework for the graph showing how much space stands for every ten degrees. Draw in bars that show the highest temperature and the lowest temperature each day. Be sure to make a key that explains which bar shows high temperature and which shows low temperature. Then use your graph to summarize facts about the weather.

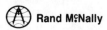 **Rand McNally**

ACTIVITY 2: Interpreting a Bar Graph

A bar graph holds a lot of information, so you can use it to learn many things. In this activity you will use a bar graph to answer questions and then write about what you learn from the graph.

Development:

This graph shows the average monthly temperature in North City over one year. Study the graph to decide what the weather is usually like in North City. Also look for changes that take place at different times of the year.

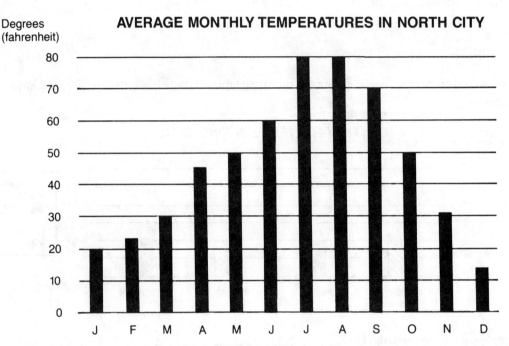

1. A farmer wants to plant crops in the spring, but must wait until the temperature is at least 50°. When can that farmer plant the crops? _____

2. The river in North City is frozen when the temperature is below 26°. In which months is the river frozen?

_____

3. Write three facts about the climate in North City that are shown on the graph

_____

_____

_____

Application:

Write a paragraph that summarizes what you learned about North City from the graph. Be sure to write a good topic sentence that summarizes what you want to say. Then support it with facts from the graph. Write your paragraph below.

_____

_____

_____

_____

_____

_____

_____

Rand McNally

ACTIVITY 3: Applying Information from a Bar Graph

You can use the facts shown on a bar graph in many ways. In this activity you will use facts about ice cream to decide what flavors you will make.

Development:

This graph shows the number of ice cream cones of four different flavors sold at the Penguin Ice Cream Store in one day. Study the graph and then answer the questions below.

True - False

Put F for statements that are false, T for statements that are true.

1. _____ People bought 40 chocolate ice cream cones.

2. _____ No one bought vanilla ice cream cones.

3. _____ People bought more almond fudge than maple nut ice cream cones.

4. _____ More people bought chocolate ice cream cones.

Application:

You are the owner of the Penguin Ice Cream Store. You want to decide how much of each flavor you will make for the week. First, make a bar graph that shows what you expect to sell of each flavor for the whole week. That graph will show you how much of each flavor you will need.

How would the following changes affect your sales?

(A) The weather gets much hotter.

(B) The weather gets much colder.

Make other graphs to show how much ice cream you would expect to sell if either of those changes took place.

ACTIVITY 4: Making a Bar Graph

Now you are ready to make your own bar graph.

Development:

There is an open graph on this page. It will show the number of new homes a builder finished in four years. Use the following information to fill in the graph.

Number of homes built:

1981: 40 homes   1982: 50 homes   1983: 15 homes   1984: 20 homes

Now draw the same information on this bar graph. Be careful, you need to find a place between 40 and 60 to show 50 and a place near 20 to show 15.

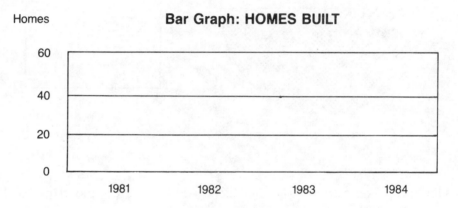

1. In which year did the builder build the most homes? _____

2. One year the builder thought about getting into a different business. Which year do you think that was? _____

3. One year the builder had to hire more workers. In which year did the builder hire the most workers? _____

Application:

Make a bar graph to show facts about part of your community. It could be the number of different kinds of stores, which you can find out by using the yellow pages in the phone directory. Count the number of stores that sell shoes, records, ice cream, balloons, and any other product you like. Then show the number by making a bar graph.

After you make your bar graph, write questions that would help someone explain what the graph shows about your community.

CHAPTER 3: Circle Graphs

Circle or pie graphs are used to show parts of a whole. The circle stands for 100%, or the entire thing. Each smaller piece represents a part of the whole. In this section you will learn how to use circle graphs.

ACTIVITY 1: Finding Facts in a Circle Graph

This circle graph shows facts about rainfall in a city.

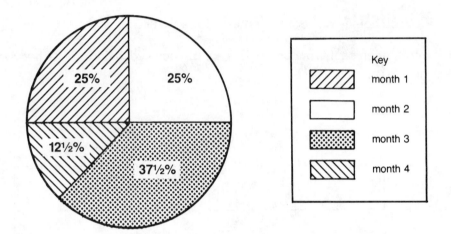

Development:

The circle stands for the total rainfall in City B (eight inches) during one four-month period. Each piece represents one month. Month 1 had two inches of rain (25% or 1/4); month 2 had 2 inches of rain (25% or 1/4); month 3 had 3 inches of rain (37 1/2% or a little more than 1/3); month 4 had one inch of rain (12 1/2% or a little more than 1/10).

1. Which month had the least rain? _____

2. Which month had the most rain? _____

3. In which two months did the city get one-fourth of the total rain for the four months?

_____ and _____

Application:

Write one sentence about each month and include at least one fact about the month that the graph shows.

1. _____

2. _____

3. _____

4. _____

ACTIVITY 2: Interpreting Information from a Circle Graph

Circle graphs show how something is divided into shares. People also call them pie graphs because they look like pies cut into pieces. Here is a pie graph about pies. It shows the different kinds of pies people ate at a restaurant in one week.

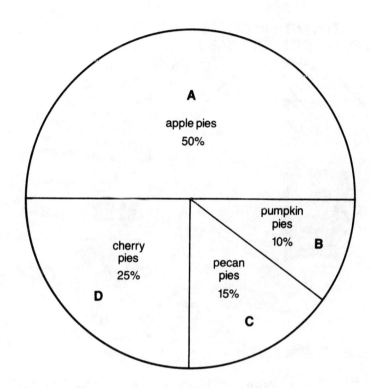

Development:

Write the letter of the kind of pie that each of these statements describes.

1. _____ People ate the smallest number of this kind of pie.

2. _____ People ate more of these pies than any other kind of pie.

3. _____ Half a circle graph stands for 50%. Of the pies people ate, 50% were this kind of pie.

4. _____ One-quarter of a circle graph stands for 25%. Which kind of pie is 25% of the total?

5. _____ and _____. Two kinds of pies did not sell as well as the others; the restaurant sold less than 25% of each of these pies. Which ones were these?

Application:

Use the facts to summarize the restaurant's pie sales. Determine how many pies of each kind the restaurant sold if they sold a total of 100 pies.

_____ apple _____ pumpkin _____ cherry _____ pecan

 **Rand McNally**

ACTIVITY 3: Applying Information from a Circle Graph

This graph shows where students in one social studies class were born. Remember that half of a circle graph stands for 50%, or one half of the total, and a quarter stands for 25%, or one-fourth of the total.

**STUDENTS IN ONE
SOCIAL STUDIES CLASS**

Students born in:

Chula Vista

National City

San Diego

Coronado

Development:

Use the graph to answer the following questions.

1. There are 28 students in the class. How many of them were born in San Diego? _____

2. How many of them were born in Coronado? _____

3. What is the combined number of students born in National City and Chula Vista? _____

4. What per cent of the students were born in San Diego? _____

5. If 75% of the students were born in San Diego, how many would that be? _____

6. Which city is the birthplace of the most students? _____

7. The class plans a field trip to the birthplace of the fewest members of the class. Which city will they visit? _____

Application:

Collect the following information about students in your class: how many blocks they travel to school each day, what kinds of sandwiches they like, or any other interesting fact. Then make circle graphs showing the percentage of students in each grouping. For example, you could show different kinds of pizza and the percentage of students that likes each kind.

ACTIVITY 4: Analyzing Information in Circle Graphs

After you get the facts from a graph, you should decide what those facts tell you about the part of the world they represent.

Development:

The following graphs show a big change in labor—the way people work—in the United States. Examine the graphs, then answer the questions that follow.

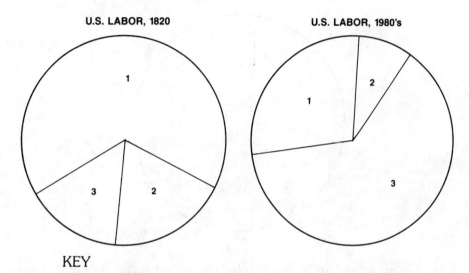

U.S. LABOR, 1820

U.S. LABOR, 1980's

KEY

1 People who work in farming, forestry, fishing and mining

2 People who work in factories

3 People who work in service jobs

1. Which graph shows that about 65% of the workers have service jobs?

_____ 1820's _____ 1980's

2. What kinds of changes in the United States might have led more workers to become factory workers than farmers?

_____ There was more and more farm land.

_____ There were more factories.

_____ There were more people to feed.

Application:

Analyze the graphs. What do they tell about the kinds of changes in work in the United States since 1820? Write three sentences that tell changes you think are important.

A. _____

B. _____

C. _____

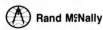 Rand McNally

ACTIVITY 5: Making Circle Graphs

Now that you know how to use a circle graph, make one of your own.

Development:

Make a circle graph showing these facts about the kinds of pets sold last week. Total number of pets sold: 20; dogs: 10; cats: 5; rabbits: 3; hamsters: 2.

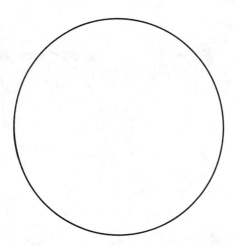

Application:

Here is some information about exports from a country. (An export is a product that one country sells to another.) Show this information in a circle graph. Then write questions about the facts shown by the graph. Your questions should begin by asking for the facts. Then you should write questions that ask people to think about those facts. For example you could ask what kind of work many people probably have in the country of Farmia.

Exports from the country of Farmia:

minerals: 10%	farm machinery: 25%
agricultural products: 40%	automobiles 25%

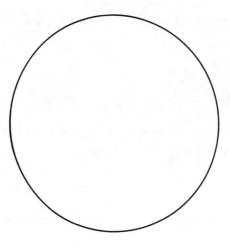

Chapter 4: Line Graphs

A line graph uses the same kind of framework as a bar graph, but instead of showing information with a bar, it shows amounts with a point. The graph then uses a line to join all those points. In this section you will learn how to read a line graph.

Activity 1: Reading a Line Graph

The simplest type of line graph shows only one kind of information. The graph on this page shows the pounds of pecans shelled in one week.

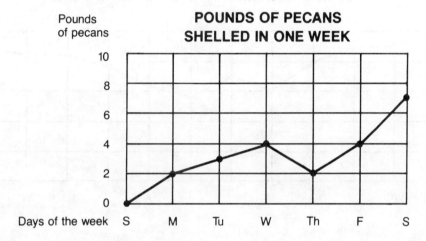

Development:

The vertical lines stand for the days of the week. The horizontal lines stand for the pounds of pecans shelled in the one-week period. Use the graph to check the following facts. Look to see if the numbers are correct. At least one number below is incorrect. Fix any errors, then fill in the missing numbers.

Sunday: 0 pounds   Thursday: 3 pounds

Monday: 5 pounds   Friday: ____ pounds

Tuesday: 3 pounds   Saturday: 7 pounds

Wednesday: ____ pounds

TOTAL: 22 pounds

Application:

Write four facts about the pecan production for this one week.

Write one sentence for each fact.

1. _____

2. _____

3. _____

4. _____

ACTIVITY 2: Interpreting a Line Graph

People use line graphs to show differences between parts of a situation and to show changes over time. These line graphs show differences and changes.

Development:

In this activity you will begin with a line graph that shows changes in rainfall in one place. Then you will use line graphs to contrast changes in rainfall in two different places.

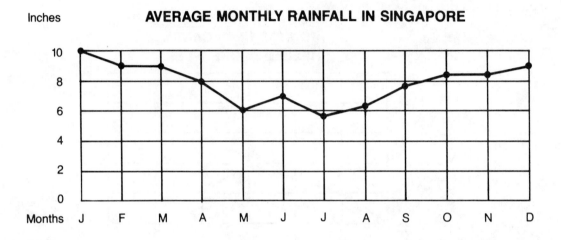

This graph shows the average monthly rainfall in Singapore. Study the graph and answer these questions about it.

1. In which four month period does the least amount of rain fall?

   from _____ through _____

2. Which month has the most rainfall? _____

3. Which month has the least amount of rainfall? _____

4. During which months does the amount of rainfall increase over the previous month?

   _____

   _____

   _____

   _____

   _____

5. Write two sentences that summarize information about the rainfall in Singapore shown by this graph.

A. _____

B. _____

You can show more than one set of information on a line graph, so you can use a line graph to compare information. To show that different lines stand for different things, you can use different colors or solid and dotted lines. This line graph shows the rainfall in the two cities.

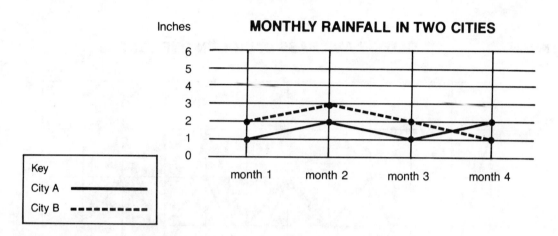

You can see differences on the line graph.

6. Which city got more rain in Month 2? _____

   In Month 4? _____

7. You can see similarities, too. In which month did both cities get more rainfall than the month before that?

   _____

8. In which month did both cities get less rain than the month before? _____

Application:

Make a line graph to show how well two different teams are doing. You could show the scores of one of your school's teams and another team, or you could show the scores of professional teams. Your line graph will not show how many games the teams won, but it will show how many points they scored. So you will have to make another graph to show how many games they won or lost. Instead of making another line graph, make a circle graph that shows the percentage of games they won and lost. Then put the two graphs together and add some sentences to explain what they show about the teams. You can add pictures and other information to turn these graphs into part of a book you make about the teams.

ACTIVITY 3: Summarizing a Line Graph

This graph shows facts about fish caught by two different people. They went fishing every month for twelve months, and they caught two different kinds of fish.

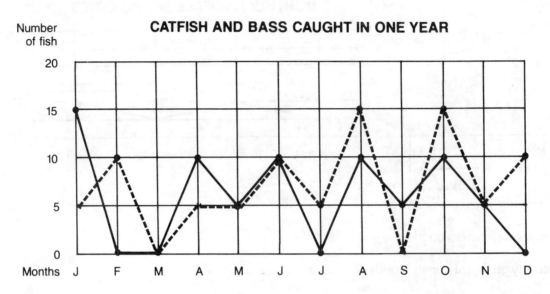

Development:

Use the facts from the graph to answer these questions. For questions 1-8 write T if it is true, F if it is false.

1. _____ They caught more catfish than bass during the year.

2. _____ They caught more fish in June, July and August than in December, January and February.

3. _____ They caught the same number of catfish and bass in May.

4. _____ They caught more catfish than bass every month.

5. _____ May is the best month to catch catfish.

6. _____ Winter is the worst season to go fishing.

7. _____ It is easier to catch bass than catfish in January.

8. _____ If you want to catch catfish, the best time is in September.

Application:

Make a plan for fishing. You have only four months during the year to go fishing. Choose the four months you plan to fish and tell the kinds of fish you expect to catch in those months.

Month   Fish

_____   _____

_____   _____

_____   _____

_____   _____

Now make your line graph.

ACTIVITY 4: Making a Line Graph

You can make your own line graph if you know facts about a situation that changes over time.

Development:

Make a line graph that shows the average temperatures in the imaginary town of Farmville. You get to make up the temperatures and then show them on a graph.

First what are the average high and low temperatures there? (You need to show the low temperatures as well as the high ones because the farmers of Farmville need to plan when to plant their crops, and they cannot plant them when it is below freezing.)

	high	low		high	low
January			February		
March			April		
May			June		
July			August		
September			October		
November			December		

Draw your temperature graph here. Use a line to show the highs and another line to show the lows. Be sure to make a key for the graph.

Application:

Use your graph of Farmville to make a plan for a farmer who lives there. Plan the farmer's planting schedule and harvest schedule. Also decide when the farmer might take a vacation. Based on the kind of climate you choose for Farmville, send the farmer to a place with a very different kind of climate for that vacation.

Part Three/
Developing Skills with Charts, Tables, and Time Lines

When you use a chart, table, or time line you *see* many things at the same time—how many pizzas people ate, how long it took to build a castle, or what time it is in Paris. You can read facts in paragraphs, but if you have many facts you have to read many paragraphs. Charts, tables, and time lines can save time if you know how to use them. In Part 3 you will learn how to use facts from charts, tables, and time lines.

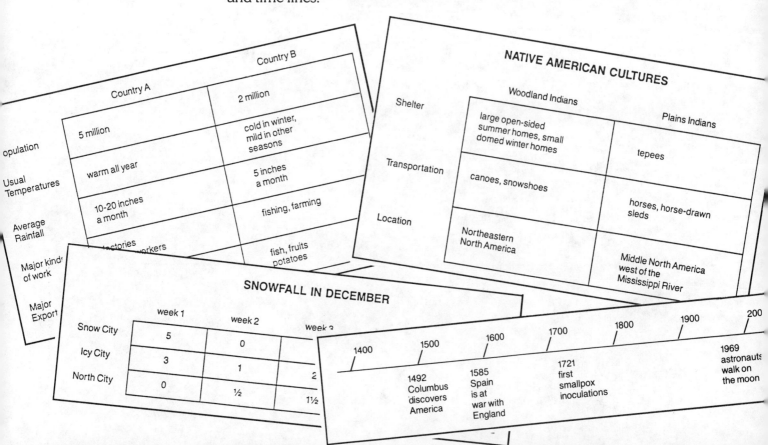

CHAPTER 1: Interpreting Facts in Tables

People use tables for the same reason they use graphs to make information clearer. In this section you will learn how to find and use facts in tables.

ACTIVITY 1: Finding Facts in Tables

Tables can show many kinds of information, and they usually use numbers as well as words to show those facts. The following table shows the amount of snowfall in three cities during December. It is an imaginary table, because the cities are not real places. But people at weather bureaus in real cities keep this kind of information. They often use tables to show how the weather is changing.

SNOWFALL IN DECEMBER

	week 1	week 2	week 3	week 4	total
Snow City	5	0	1	3	9
Icy City	3	1	2	4	10
North City	0	½	1½	2	4

Development:

Which city fits each statement? Write the name of the city on the line after each sentence.

1. This city had no snowfall in the second week of December.

_____

2. This city had four inches of snow in the fourth week of December.

_____

3. This city had more and more snow each week in December.

_____

4. This city did not have to use its snow plows the first week in December.

_____

5. This city had the most snow in the month of December.

_____

6. This city had the least snow in the month of December.

_____

Application:

Based on this table, write a paragraph about one city.

 **Rand McNally**

ACTIVITY 2: Interpreting a Table

Tables make it easy to find information quickly. Turn this news report into a table to show the difference between finding information in a table and in a written report. It reports the types of damage in four wards (parts) of Bay City after a major storm.

News Report: There was a big storm in the Bay City area last night. Today as the cleanup began, different wards reported different problems. In Ward 1 the fire station said that five homes had been burned, that the tornado had ripped siding from three other homes, and that hail had broken windows on twelve homes. Ward 2 was luckier. No homes were burned. The tornado did crush two garages. Hail damage was minor, with two homes damaged. Ward 3 was the worst hit with damage. Twenty homes had broken windows from the hail. Six homes had tornado damage, and four had fire damage. Ward 4 was badly hit, too. Seven homes had fires, sixteen had tornado damage, and five homes have windows boarded up due to hail damage.

Development:

Fill in the table with information from the news report. Then answer the questions below.

HOUSE DAMAGE REPORTED IN BAY CITY

houses damaged by:	Ward 1	Ward 2	Ward 3	Ward 4	Totals
Fire					
Tornado					
Hail					
Totals					

1. Which ward reported the most damage? _____

2. Which ward had no fire damage? _____

3. Did fire or hail do more damage? _____

4. The mayor did not visit one ward because that ward had so little damage. Which ward did not get a visit

   from the mayor?_____

Application:

Make a table that shows facts about your community. It should show facts about the kinds of businesses there. To complete your table, you will need to use the yellow pages to find out how many different businesses are in the community.

ACTIVITY 3: Analyzing Information in a Table

A table can make it easy to contrast different things because it gives you the facts quickly.

Development:

The table shows rainfall in two very different cities: Detroit, Michigan, and Manaus, Brazil. Detroit is a city far north in North America. Manaus is a city in South America along the Amazon River. The two cities have very different climates. It is warm all year in Manaus, and Detroit has hot weather in summer, cold weather in winter. Study the table below and then contrast the climate in Detroit and Manaus.

RAINFALL IN TWO CITIES

	J	F	M	A	M	J	J	A	S	O	N	D
Detroit, Michigan U.S.A.	2"	2"	3"	3"	3"	4"	3"	2"	2"	2"	2"	2"
Manaus, Brazil	8"	8"	8"	9"	7"	4"	2"	2"	2"	4"	4"	8"

Write a summary of the differences between the climates of the two cities based on information shown in the table.

_____

_____

_____

_____

_____

Application:

Look back through the graph section of this workbook and find facts about two different places. Make a table showing those facts. Write a summary of the differences between places shown on your table, just as you did for Manaus and Detroit.

CHAPTER 2: Tracing History on Time Lines

Time lines help show the order in which things happened. You can also use a time line to see how far apart events are in time. Time lines are especially useful in studying history.

ACTIVITY 1: Getting Facts from a Time Line

Look at this time line of one person's history.

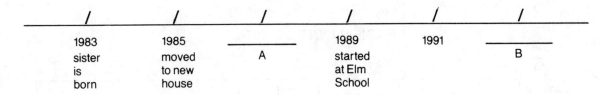

Development:

This time line is divided into two-year periods. What years should go into the blanks? Fill them in with the correct years.

Time lines can cover many years. This time line is divided into ten year periods, or decades. Fill in the blanks on this time line.

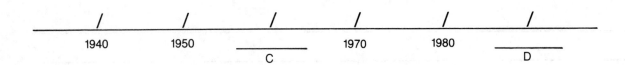

Some time lines deal with centuries. Each part of this time line stands for a century, or 100 years. What years should go in the blanks? Fill them in.

Application:

Make a time line for your own lifetime. Include important events in your life and things that have happened in the United States during your life-time.

ACTIVITY 2: Interpreting a Time Line

Some time lines include the year "0" which is a dividing point used to identify the years before and after the birth of Christ.

Years before "0" are called B.C. and we count those years backward. For example, 100 B.C., 75 B.C., 50 B.C., 25 B.C., 0; so the century before "0" is 100 B.C.

Years after "0" are counted forward and are called A.D. For example, 0, 25 A.D., 50 A.D., 75 A.D., 100 A.,D.; so the century after "0" is 100 A.D.

Development:

A. Tell how this time line is divided:

_____ into 5-year periods   _____ into 10-year periods

_____ into 15-year periods   _____ into 25-year periods

B. & C. Fill in the blanks on the time line.

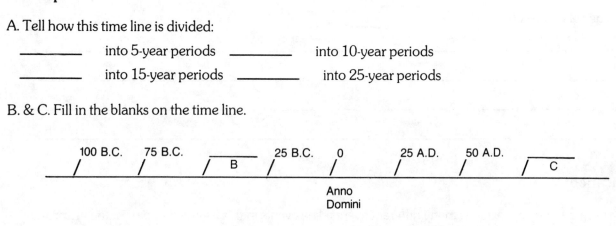

The next time line shows centuries B.C. and A.D. Study it, then answer the questions.

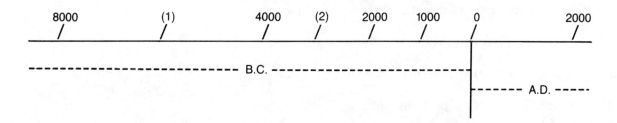

1. How many centuries does this time line show? _____

2. What is the correct year for Point 1? _____

3. What is the correct year for Point 2? _____

4. How many years apart are Points 1 and 2? _____

There is a similarity between two of the events on the time line on the following page. Look for events that have a connection (are alike in some special way). Then explain that connection.

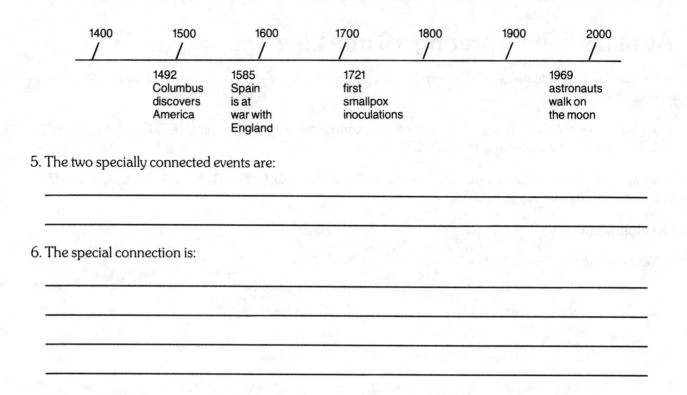

5. The two specially connected events are:

_____

_____

6. The special connection is:

_____

_____

_____

_____

Application:

A time period in history includes many different events. The events in this list that are part of the history of one city—Chicago. Find the four events that tell about improving transportation. Then make a Chicago transportation time line with those four events.

1837—Charles Morgan starts the first Chicago furniture factory.

1833—The population is about 350.

1834—The first steamboat to travel in Chicago arrives.

1831—The first Chicago River bridge is built.

1834—John Beaubien brings the first piano to Chicago.

1832—A lighthouse is built.

1836—The first Chicago flour mill opens.

1835—The first Chicago library opens.

1840—A bridge is built at Clark Street.

1838—Samuel Morse invents the Morse code.

1839—The first daily newspaper in Chicago starts.

ACTIVITY 3: Making a Time Line—A Special Project

People have created many different inventions throughout history. Use this list of important inventions to make a time line. Then choose one date from your time line that you think was very important because of the inventions made at that time. Write a paragraph explaining why those inventions made that time period the most important part of the entire time line.

1857—The first public elevator is installed.

1888—George Eastman introduces the roll film and the box camera.

1855—Karl Benz invents the automobile.

1884—E. Waterman invents the fountain pen.

1925—The flashbulb for photography is invented.

1867—Christopher Sholes invents the typewriter.

1903—The Wright brothers fly the first powered airplane.

1927—The first "talking picture" is made.

1907—The first helicopter flight takes place.

1877—Thomas Edison invents the phonograph.

1855—The first artificial plastic is invented.

1886—People learn how to make aluminum.

1924—Clarence Birdseye introduces frozen foods.

1879—The light bulb is invented.

1876—Alexander Graham Bell patents the telephone.

These aren't all the inventions. You can find out more about inventions by reading about them in the encyclopedia. After you find out more about inventions, make another time line showing what you have learned.

CHAPTER 3: Comparing and Contrasting with Charts

A chart is a tool used to show facts clearly. Charts always have headings to explain what is shown.
Some charts have headings at the top as well as at the side. As you work on these activities, you will learn how to use the headings and facts in a chart to discover important things about the world.

ACTIVITY 1: Finding Information in a Chart

The first thing to do when you see a chart is to read the headings, which show what the chart describes. Then you should study it to learn about that topic.

Development:

You can use a chart to show any kind of facts about a topic. In this activity you will use two different charts to learn some of the ways charts can show facts.

TOURIST ATTRACTIONS

Chicago	Los Angeles	New York
Sears Tower	Disneyland	Statue of Liberty
Lake Michigan	Universal Studios	Empire State Building
Lincoln Park Zoo	La Brea Tar Pits	Rockefeller Center

1. What is the title of this chart? _____

2. What kinds of facts would you expect to find in this chart?

    _____

    _____

3. Which three cities does this chart include?

    _____

    _____

    _____

4. You will find a zoo in each of the three cities, but you will only find Rockefeller Center in one. Where will you find it?

    _____

5. Which city would you visit to see Lake Michigan? _____

NATIVE AMERICAN CULTURES

	Woodland Indians	Plains Indians
Shelter	large open-sided summer homes, small domed winter homes	tepees
Transportation	canoes, snowshoes	horses, horse-drawn sleds
Location	Northeastern North America	Middle North America west of the Mississippi River

Some charts have headings along the top and along the side, as this chart does. The headings along the side help to show how the facts are organized and make them easier to locate.

6. Find two kinds of transportation used by the Woodlands Indians.

_____ and _____.

To find that information, you used the top heading, Woodland Indians, and the side heading, Transportation. You didn't have to read the whole chart.

7. Which headings would you use to find where the Woodlands Indians lived?

_____ and _____

8. Which group used horses? _____

Which headings did you use to find that answer?

_____

Application:

Make your own chart about different places. The places could be cities in your state, places you have visited, or places you have studied. Make headings for your chart and then include facts in each category of the chart.

Activity 2: Finding and Using Facts in Charts

This chart shows facts about two different countries. You will use it in this activity and in the next activity. First you will learn facts from the chart, then you will interpret them in Activity 3.

TWO COUNTRIES

	Country A	Country B
Population	5 million	2 million
Usual Temperatures	warm all year	cold in winter, mild in other seasons
Average Rainfall	10-20 inches a month	5 inches a month
Major kinds of work	factories, service workers	fishing, farming
Major Exports	machinery, grain	fish, fruits potatoes

Development:

Use the information in the chart to answer the questions about the countries.

1. Which country has a climate that is mild and rainy? _____

2. Which country has cold winters? _____

3. Which country exports different kinds of foods? _____

4. Which country has many service workers? _____

Application:

What facts can you find about different parts of your own country? Look for facts about these regions: the northeast, the northwest, the southeast, the southwest, and the midwest. List the facts, then make a chart with these headings: climate, products, important cities.

The Northeast

_____

_____

_____

The Northwest

_____

_____

_____

The Southeast

_____

_____

_____

The Southwest

_____

_____

_____

The Midwest

_____

_____

_____

CHART ON REGIONS

ACTIVITY 3: Interpreting Information in a Chart

Once you find the facts in a chart, you are ready to use those facts. In Activity 3, you will use facts in the chart for Activity 2 to learn more about the two countries.

Development:

The following questions ask you to use facts from the chart in Activity 2 to tell about the two countries. After you read the question, you will have to look for information, and then you will have to think about those facts to answer the question.

1. Which country probably has more cities? _____

   What facts did you use to answer this question? _____

   _____

2. Which country probably has more farms? _____

   What facts did you use to answer this question? _____

   _____

3. What might Country B import from Country A? _____

   What facts did you use to answer this question? _____

   _____

4. What might Country A import from Country B? _____

   What facts did you use to answer this question? _____

   _____

Application:

Invent another country—Country C. Add it to the chart. Then make up more questions based on comparing and contrasting the three countries in the chart. Write answers to your own questions.

_____

_____

_____

_____

_____

_____

_____

_____

ACTIVITY 4: Charting Your Community—A Special Project

Make a chart that shows important facts about your community. Use this framework to organize your chart. You can make a much bigger chart, including pictures you collect, or you can draw pictures to show each of these parts of your community.

Climate

_____

_____

Kinds of
Homes

_____

_____

_____

_____

Kinds of
Transportation

_____

_____

_____

_____

Recreation

_____

_____

_____

_____

Add other categories—what else is important to show about your community?

_____

_____

_____

_____

_____

_____

_____

_____

_____

_____

CHART OF MY COMMUNITY